don't think about it and you'll be fine

torrye's book of poems and other nonsense

(poems)

Victoria Marie LaFlamme

Cover Art | Victoria Marie LaFlamme

Book Design | Mitch Green

| ISBN 978-0-578-83434-4 |

Blog | queenofcrows.blogspot.com |

This book is dedicated to my Papa. Thank you for my melon head and always making me smile. Love you to death and beyond.

......stay weird

smaller than a pocket poem.

Walnuts dancing on chairs with berries
and birds,
                The air is delicate with hints of
orange and ginger.
Christmas night is lovely, while the fire
crackles and the children giggle.

poem (two)

I'm sorry I was nowhere to be found
That day in the middle of May
I stepped outside and I never made
My way back home
I needed some time
I needed some rest
The air felt so nice
It was such a delight
I couldn't stop myself
I couldn't help
But think of angels
Weeping, while we
Danced our night
Away to classical music
And red wine

~~tangerines.~~

who have i become with
you by my side.
i can't take the person inside-
have to hide my thoughts- i can't
stand myself. i've given you my all-
drained of sins and everything. i
can't keep up with the silence.
screaming from within. my
heart asks for help. my soul
wants a home, not a temporary
fix. i can't stand the room.

A dozen agate roses.

Wilting away, my love seeps into your bad dreams.
Nightmares of peach-less trees and white noise.
You leave footprints behind as your shadow follows.

Poem.

Perhaps it's hard to breathe because
the
Love inside my soul suffocates my body
whole. Bigger than the earth, deeper
than a tree:
I will always love.

Winter is my soul.

As thick as porcelain snow,

My wings continue to grow.

With summer thoughts in the

Dead of Winter- snow falls

From my mind. The inside is

Warm, with the crackle of

An evergreen fire.

start the procession line, I think I
have died.

It kills me to say goodbye
But what really hits my soul
Is feeling alone when we are
Together

Your smile lights up a room
I envy your nose and
Perfect teeth
Those green eyes could
Save my soul-

But my time here is up
I've been stuck in this
Cage for far too long
And I've finally realized-

Life is about being
Happy with yourself,
With your soul-
To create your imagination
Into reality and just go

At first I never thought
I could be alone
I thought I needed someone
To hold and call home

But come to find out,
The world isn't as scary as
I thought

Or maybe I grew stronger-

The stars whispered to me
One night, while trying
To fall asleep,

*It's Ok to let go, to make a better
you.....*
This version of Torrye has expired.

~~EJECT.~~

poem

I listen to the moon,
I take notes when the seasons
change.
My heart belongs to my backyard river.
When the clouds rush in anxiety
reaches my teeth,
to bring me higher than
The sky before the wind waves me
goodbye.
I take it in, when I hear the tree growing.
GROWING,
G R O W I N G.

Put it in your pocket.

To eat the laughter from your smile
  Time slips with raindrops that splatter
    Upon the forehead of the unborn
child

When the birds cry.

I don't like it when it's cold
        Inside my heart-
No noise, no sound, no soul.
I don't like it when it's cold
        With a mind full of snow
And a late summer-
I couldn't imagine spring with no
Flowers.
        Set the table, set the flowers.
In the dirt we play, while mother slaves
away
        In the kitchen, where love is made
And formed into edible surprises.
Forks on the left, spoons on the right.
Remember: Forks on the left,
Spoons on the right.

pocket poem 006.

Remember when the spring mornings
lasted a lifetime?
And the sun would shine through our fog
filled minds-
Where the trees dance and the sky is a
kind of ocean blue.

poem 13.

The glow of Jupiter's Moon/
The sound of the Ocean's voice/
The color of the December sky/
The echo of the Crow's cry/

Kiss my scars, bring me home and tuck me into the river.

Sing me to sleep while the moonlight seeps into my skin.

Kiss my forehead goodnight while I drift away.

Evaporate
This love
Fallen
To the ground
Broken
Into
Pieces
That
Cannot
Be glued back
Together
A place where
We used to sleep
Now a
Place where
My nightmares
Dance and sing
I can't take
The pain
Of this
Feeling

....

Numb, a kind of cold

poem for your soul (or pocket)

Honey stuck to my brain, melting like ice
on a muggy day.
(Swaying back and forth)
Melting down the drain, my love has
expired like your desire.
(Swaying back and forth)
Sucking on dreams with no rain is like
dancing with no feet.
(Swaying back and forth)

nothing.

small as dust
sip of the moon
gold in her eyes

watch the moon follow us

If you travel with stones in
your pockets how do you float home?
When the river water rises,
where do the tree roots grow?
After the sun falls asleep
and the stars shine,
Where does the moon hide?

1 thirteen 3.

the sky seems like a good place to hide
our dreams.
the trees and their bees can hold my
secrets.
i feel free when my toes touch the dirt
and the sun
          shines
                    down
                              on
                                   me.

dreaming of the day...

Singing softly to him
  As he kisses my nose
Write our love in the night sky
Diamonds and coffee
Reading and writing
While he plays me morning
Melodies I sip my tea
And just cry
The silent snow falls outside

Clouds with a cold.

Sipping love off your lips while my body
is hung out to dry.
On the line, it hangs for days. The
breeze hits it *g e n t l y .*
Kiss my mind: the dreams disappear as
months end.
At the riverbed I begin to build a bird's
nest.

I think I'm ready to shed this skin.
Worn in, like that sun-bleached tee-
Tattered, like parts of me are missing
Hanging on to what seems to exist but doesn't-
Numb, so numb I can't even feel the snow.
This skin I've worn, for the past decade is torn,
Ragged, faded into oblivion where you don't exist.
I think I'm ready to conquer this world:
Book in hand, words in my mind, me: alone.
But that's ok, I am the Queen of this Kingdom
Anyways. I have found my way, I can trust myself
More than ever. I know when it feels like it's time-
Let me go, let my scent to the woods and forget
My name. I think I'm ready to shed this skin.

24.

Silence sleeps upon the broken rose
petals,
The men weep before they enter the
church.
Twenty-four days and still no sign of life.

twenty-five.

Honey dew dripping
    Off of lips I've kissed.
With a charcoal heart, nothing left to
Lose besides you.

Pearls

pears and ginger ale,
spirits from above.
as i pick through the
newspaper, as i read
through the obituaries.
where are YOU
in regards to *this love?*

very small pocket poem.

When a pen is held to my brain:
Your words, they slip down the drain.
Like silk against my thighs, light and
delicate.
Eyes full of lies and lilies- smell the fresh
December air.

Watching time set into another day.
Things like grass and trees make my
        Soul sing-
lullabies to the stars and moon for
someone must put them to sleep too-

Dead Numbers Painted on the Sky.

I wish I could paint like my great
grandfather Frank.
Graceful colors blend together, melting
the mind.
Dainty: As the paintbrush softly dances
across the paper.

a dinner poem.

What a waste of time you are, selling
me your soul for a
Bucket full of knees. You make me
dance around the
Living room when no one is home,
before dinner in
Between plates and spoons.

asking for forgiveness
holding onto a broken branch
eating a sour lime
trumpets playing
in the background
i am still blind

leave me alone if you want me
to be ~~happy~~

Happiness is cutting my tongue on
a rose thorn
And eating the midnight stars.

Happiness is being alone in the
mysterious dark   woods,
When no one is
around and
it's easy
to breathe.

Poem 017.

She smells like the mountain air and
dances with the wind-
She lets the birds do her hair while the
trees hold her sins-
On top of the world she sits with her
toes dipped in the sunrise-

four walls.

I wouldn't mind
If you took a slice
Of my mind
With the quiver
Of winter
And the love for
A sunrise

...
as
lovers,
we
must
watch
one
another
grow
~

Pocket poem (love)

by the grace of this sun and the moon
gods, i
met
you
and you've loved me ever since

butterfly

When the butterfly dies, who takes the
time
To clean their wings?

When the butterfly dies, who takes the
time
To bury their soul?

When the butterfly dies, who takes the
time
To let the others know?

poem

i will love
you like the
sky loves the
sun. like the
moon loves the stars.
with all my soul:
everything to give,
all yours.

a baby

When the snow covers the cemetery
before dawn
When the rain falls oh so softly on my
face
When the smell of flowers bring joy to
the soul
I will love you once more

typewriter thoughts

when was the last time
you went to the dentist?

a sour hypocrite, you
shave woodchips into

the minds of unborn
children-

you never answer
your front door. why?

sleepwalking lovers come out to play,
all i see is their shadows

For him.

I want to spend the rest of my midnight
moons with you.
I want to lick the words from your
tongue.
I want to love you until there are no
more tomorrows.

years have passed and now you're here

Intertwined, you and i
   Our minds: seek redemption, seek
saving
I fear the fact *I love the old you*,
   I fear this feeling could turn stale,
quick. But maybe you've
Stayed the same and I was the one that
changed. Had to grow:
Bloom, like lilacs in the dead of
summer. *Hot July*. I had to
Realize what was in front of my eyes. To
seek the
Company of love and want your
warmth. To know what it's like
      To really feel *love*.
            Just tell me you still love me,
hold me closer than life itself.
Show me how to feel again, cus I've
grown numb. It's time for
My rebirth: *a new me, a new world*. I am
scared. I've seen only seas but I can
Hear the city screaming my name. Take
my heart and tell me
Everything will be ok.

44.

comfort found
on the petals
of rose
thorns thrown
to the ocean's
floor

Jasmine fields.

As I brush against the thorn of this rose,
          Trickle down the spine of your
mind.
Blood: Warm as a light, dark as death.
Dripping,
D R I P P I N G,
          DROP.
Counting words, counting the time on
the CLOCK.
To start a fire you must gather your
words
          Whole, hold the candlestick to
your heart
And whisper the words of the
hummingbird.
Softer than the feather of my backyard
crow.

The white cedar branches sway and wind howls.

A Pocket Poem #2.

Take just a sliver of my mind
    and explain to me if you can tell the
time.
Hours turn into days, where days
        make months and years go by
faster
Than the wind in the sky.

Collecting dead bugs since the
second grade.

Life is a hurricane-
    & tastes like a sunflower.
With a touch of bark and the smell of
summer rain,
Pour her soul into a mug and take a sip.

Seventeenth of December.

Where the moths sleep-
Where dreamers dance and lovers
weep.
When the ice melts into a beautiful sky
abyss.
Broken Thoughts scattered, tattered
mind
Shooting stars and cold rain wine.
Making love to you is like chasing empty
Eyes down a snow-covered road.
And there is no light in sight.

~~In a past life~~

We loved one another until dawn came
up,
Dancing into the sky with our mouths
Wide open.
To express my feelings, to let the fragile
beast out. I couldn't wish upon a soul,
the amount of rain I have seen.
I have dealt with snow and dead flowers
but nothing compares to the love we
made in the summer's heat. I remember
the first
Time your silk mouth touched mine.

Memories of us stacked in my back
brain. I just can't seem to let go.

Lord knows I will never forget your
name,
Or the way your fingertips ever so gently
Ran across my skin--

I can't forget the time you made me feel
like
The Queen of the Forest, you filled my
mind with
Gentle lies of beauty and strength.

Taking us time to rekindle, all you've
ever
Gotten was a kiss from this mouth,

Before the sea came in and took you
away from me.

One day, when we meet again, when
the sail on your boat
Takes you to me...

Shivers down my spine, only to
bring back time

We once held together with hands our
mother gave us.

Can you please just speak to me, my
mind
wanders

To places it knows not to go and

I can't

Fucking
Take it.

Please tell me,
Why did you come back?

Poem.

I envy the wind that gets to touch your delicate skin.
As the sky cries-
The angels and her mind, grow brighter
From the candlestick her father gave her.

deep blue eyes.

Soak my soul in the ~~dead~~ of winter.
Wrap my body whole with the feathers
From a hawk and a blanket of snow.
Together we can ~~grow~~ the Spring
Flowers.

poem 009.

can i fall asleep
inside your mind?
tuck me in while
Jupiter watches.

skintight.

Cut my wrist with a rib cage.
Chew on souls of the dead-
November the Fourth, choke on
Holes filled with nightmares.

mornings like this.

I took the moonlight
    and hid it in a mug.
I took the sunlight
  and scattered it across the mud.

JUST FOR US.

right now

i'm in no hurry
to watch the clouds
swim by or listen to
the mountains
cry

Sailing.

Feels like we only go backwards,
All things considered.
The ocean collects tears and fears
While the boats float on happiness.

Poem

looking for someone to
just understand my soul
tell me what i need to do
how to stay alive.

I could waste away my
days chewing and chewing
But what is there in it for me?
When I can't think straight,
And the walls bleed blue.
I can't imagine the room
Without light- but lately
Nothing can make the butterfly
Fly or the baby cry

April.

the cemetery swallows my leg whole,
   while a murder of crows watch from
above.
god only knows, where the road will go,
   cars pass by like light in the winter's
night.

no name

everyone thinks i'm nuts because i can
speak to my dad in my dreams.
dead dad.
but just believe and never do
anything to harm the man and you
too shall speak to thee.

dead January

Why do the old bones
Always come back to hurt you?
Why can't they stay in their
Own space?

Why do they want to mend
Things that they broke-
Their own bones...
I was there before and you left

Me to die. Alone with
One eye. But now seven
Winters have passed and
You come knocking
On my door

You are trying to plant seeds
In that dead Torr.
Well this Torr is dead too.

I can't tell you the truth,

It's hidden under lies and cobwebs-
Hidden under surface love and
Hopeless everything...

Alone with brittle mistakes
And love that didn't lie

Where is our
Time going?
Moving forward-

Not back.

jaded.

Come to me like the trees hug their branches.
Inside your mind, a place where it's warm.
The sun shines through the skeletons, oh my.

Pebbles.

Silicon love spread sparsely
    On top of funeral homes
And tin foil teeth.

glowing a gold kind of color

Have you ever danced naked on a Full
Moon?
    Seen a lightning bug land on your
nose?
Have you ever been to the Sea right
before a storm?
    See all the bumble bees fly North?

sea dreams.

I wonder where the ocean goes when
we fall asleep.
Where do the waves dream? What do
they think?
When the sun goes down and the full
moon comes up,
who is there to say,
"I love you"
?

summer dinner roses.

The smell of Earth lingers,
    As this day must go on.
Hang the clothes on the line,
    Pick the flowers for our
Dinner bouquet.

Don't be Shy.

mountain minds.

Promising you whispers of summer
While the sun eats our time
We dance until the end

With nothing in my pocket
But a poem, wrap your mind
Around an orange and peel that

Don't waste my time
Don't ask for my permission
As for my soul is not present

As we swallow this harsh winter
Promises disappear in the cemetery
While the dead speak softly

hummingbird's dawn.

your reflection is the only thing that i can
see-
shower your love down, down to the
sea-
never know if you are alive or dead,
your eyes
don't blink and i haven't heard you
breathe.
centuries between us, kiss your rose
petal goodbye.

Why do you have such a beautiful bird?

why do you have such a beautiful bird
If you don't let her live

Her life consists of metal bars and food
Maybe some sunlight if she asks for it

(a beautiful bird shouldn't have to ask for the light, it should be given to her as a gift. As for she is a gift from another world that we should cherish and hold gently)

Such radiant colors,
Beautiful set of wings
Why do you have a bird if you
Just keep her in her cage?

Don't be greedy, don't be mean
Let her out for the world to see

She has a purpose, she serves as a symbol
Let her magnificent soul rise
And fly

Free.
(like a bird should be)

08 Pocket Poem.

My skull is full of knowledge,
my skull is full of blood.

I can see where the road is
taking me, that's why my seat belt
is on.

When the rivers meet, the
Children greet the Elderly.

Before I go home please make a
stop at my favorite Oak Tree.

smells like evergreens

Walking softly atop the snow-covered
fields
Where cows stand and the crows stare
Hear nothing but the bottom of my boots
Scrape the iced over grass

Gazing into the gray bleak sky
Clouds whisk by with confidence and
prayers
Inside the fire devours our fears and lies
While warming the children alive

e.a.r.t.h.

Crickets.
Blades
Of
Grass.
Air.
Rain.
Ants.
Dirt.
Trees.
The
Earth
Is
Beautiful.

A night away

Write our names in the midnight sky
Passing by, laughing and smiling
Melting but still cold
Dance around the planets with me
Wrap my body in that white dress
And let my hair touch the floor
Funerals are for people who
Don't have real friends, so before
We let the procession begin,
Pick some flowers from Saturn
and I will water our minds for our
time has to end.
In this life,
I have come to find out
That all good things die and
Time is all we share. So let's dance
Until our feet bleed and our hearts
Make
Love.

Impeach the Peachy Prick.

Cowardly humans seek fear out of

Children-

Shaking their minds, filling their thoughts

with

Lies and disgrace to mankind-

Politics eat their words and fill

newspapers

with lies-

With the clock ticking furiously-

While the earth says, "your time is up"

Spending their last buck on a beer,

taking

Hookers home with their wives

downstairs-

Dreaming hope will come alive in the

eyes

Of the unborn, before climate change

kills

Us all.

Three Lines

The death of our Earth, which is upon us as the nights roll into years and my mirror cracks.

Where the angels dance in the silent memories of us, the stars shine brighter than blue.

The taste of the wolf moon, the blood of our loved ones, where love once lived: alive.

back pocket poem 214577

Leave me where the angels cry
Maybe they can heal my wounds

Shoot high, higher than the sky sits

Leave me where the angels cry
Maybe they can heal my wounds

Shoot high, higher than the sky sits

Pocket poem 79.

Catch me before I fall
Before I fall into the velvet river
Before the snow caresses my nose
Catch me before the woods
Swallow my body whole
Catch me before my sorrows
Drown my soul
Into the winter abyss my
Mind gently begins to boil

for you (you know who you are)

And even if we just have this for a
moment
The taste so delicate, sits on the back of
my tongue
I want to taste it again, the sins
– you make my heart melt
  The overwhelming feeling of warmth
And life just pours out of our souls
The time together we hold, So close to
our hearts
A lifetime could be measured in years
or tears
Depending on how you look at it.
We have together, such a rare
Beautiful thing, why let anyone else in?
Precious as a stone, our love could
make
One hundred gardens grow.
All I know is you give light to the dark
And you show affection towards my
wilting
      Heart.
The spirit of home tasting nostalgic
Makes me think sick-

daydream haze.

but I can't shake the feelings I've been
Drowning in since the day we met
I can see the sun setting in your eyes
Even if I'm stuck in this daze
I can't complain about my view

Snowflakes kissing

Eating silhouettes of beautiful women
      with an ocean breeze sneeze.
Three lines of bees-
No leaves on all our trees.
Lock the windows,
December
is coming.

dust

I love you as much as the moon loves
the sun.

*The kiss of midnight bliss across my
lips-*

To you my heart sings only delicate
love.

Sicilian Honey Drop

Do you ever feel like your tears mixed
with sins are reality?
Like the feelings your heart cries at
midnight, are the feelings
That your soul feeds-
When lightning turns to gold and the
moonlight
Brings you home –
Save a sip of the Moon in the morning
mug-
Take a trip to a place that smells like
cloves and tastes like Heaven.

Insignificant

I'm not afraid of most things,
but I'm afraid of the dark.
  light coming in
    when the
      midnight
      sun
touches
her
 fingertips.

she.

She who has the soul of a fox,
    who can love deeper than a canyon.

She who has the mind of a man,
    and a body of a Goddess.

a magenta kind of red

The secrets lie within the heart of the
mind,
                                        behind
the Queen.

Secluded rose gardens whisper dreams
past midnight and onward.

Crimson love seeps through eyes of
gold,
dripping like honey down a spoon.

too young for my body
too old for him
my soul sits high in existence
as the clouds count
my tears

Exit the mind of a child
While together we shine
The pennies and dimes-
For whiskey is to be served
At my funeral while the
Birds dance and my mother
Sobs-
As trees are planted
The youth sits on the
Forest floor while
The cows are out
Of town-

carry on.

Taking time to realize
  The sheep don't fall
Far from their castles
  Nor do their prey-

Nothing seems array
When money is easy
To find because the
Backyard tree was gifted
From your Father-

But when you grow up
  In an abode full of stress
And mess: money-less
Things seems real and raw
  At such a young age
Love seemed to be the only
    way-

I don't ask for you to
Shower me in gifts or money
  All I want is to dance around
The moon, with you in hand-

Sometimes the apples taste
Like the pears, and you want
To be that sweet too.
But honey,

melons
Don't grow when the sun
Can't shine, and the love
In my mind has evaporated
Into a haze-

I just feel for the people
Who think money is
The answer to love.

Because it's certainly not

tree souls.

pinecone eyes and a rusty heart-

she pours her soul out for you on a
Sunday morning.

her roots deep in the ground, *not moving.*

5689.

Where the children play,
the old man hays and his dog has three
legs.

Here the river flows upstream and
the grass grows longer between our
toes.

Don't be fooled by Peter the Farmer,
he has more horses than you think.

Pocket Poem 94.

Softer than the sea.
I cherish every kiss we share.
As the sun sets into the
horizon our hearts begin to dance.

QUEEN OF CROWS
(depends on the day)

eating the moonlight
a feeling of...
eternal love
  maybe love?
Can't describe the mess
Unfading, fading BUT
so BRIGHT
Everlasting lust
Enduring the future
With thorns sticking
Out my side

Wings spread across
  The sky
Ready to fly

Being a Queen:
  Queen of Crows,
Stars kiss me when
No one else can hold
Me

Loving me is loving
The Black:
no time
No destination

No shapes
  Just black

So before you pull
Out your sword,
The Queen of Crows
ALWAYS asks,

  Consider the time before we shared
the
Midnight sky, did you even know
I was there ?

poem

rip my skin
tear my tongue
let my words live
for the cities and the nuns
when rivers bleed human blood
bring to thee my severed thumb

01.

free your mind:
hold your soul &
taste the sky.

If you took the time
To really read through
The cattail reeds
You could find the
Sun rises brighter
On the East –

I can't stand the smell
Of the men
Who don't read
Their books
You have eyes
You have a mind
Why don't you read?
You've got all this time
I can't stand the smell
Of the men
Who don't read
Their books

Feeling my feelings.

Can you tell me why my heart bleeds
so hard,
When the diamonds fall from the Full
Moon Sky?
Can you express the feelings deep down
inside,
That hit me harder than an ocean's tide?
Why do I cry when the sky turns grey,
when
The cold rain is here to stay?
Why do I cry when I hear a mother bird
Sing to a nest full of babies?
When the winter is harsh, my frail
Soul sinks into a careless sleep
Where mountains sing to thee.
Why does it feel like my body is on
Fire when we speak?
When words make sentences
And weeks turn into slaves for the
months
To come, I can hear the church bell in
the
Distance.

LSD Love.

Do you even know how
I felt the day you left me?
When the November rain
Smelt like Heaven and
Your Mother said my name.
Where do you think I went
When you just got up and left?
I loved you. I love you. I still do.
I promise a World of Sins for
Your right hand.

A list of Living

The breath of a baby
The sound of the sun rising
The smell of a book
The taste of coffee
An old weathered touch

Rocks and waves that crash.

You want to feel me breathe?
Just bend down to the river's edge
And take that all in. That's me.

arrows.

i am here to see you whole
bare to the bone,
naked from the truth-
i am here to figure you out-
newborn face,
a heart: empty.
NOTHING inside.

Can you tell
When you grin
That I am falling
Out of my skin
The bones they hold
Before my mind
Slips I can't get a grip
Can you tell when you
Grin I want to eat the sins
I want to stop the madness
And just let love
In

Salt Water Blue.

Cast light upon her eyes,

The sea simmers in the back.

Her chest touches my heart-

Her eyes eat me whole.

Enhance the environment with

Flowers planted from love.

Embellish the soul with

Wisdom, before your

Teeth let loose.

Isolate the Sunlight, so I can feel
beautiful again.

The desire to eat your mouth.
Sweet Bitterness, your body brings-
  My soul, washed up on the ocean's
floor
Before the ~~Moon~~ could rise, before the
Stars could shine. Find time for us.
Finding time for us, is like waiting for
Heaven
To rain, waiting for the train to take me
Far, Far away, before love existed.

  Just so I COULD breathe again. I
can't feel
My toes, and I haven't eaten in a week
or so.
The knots in my stomach are tied tighter
Than my shoelaces. If I could go back in
time,
To store our time, kind of hold it: frozen.
Like a statue: can't move.
  I just want to feel you in the winter's
night.

I want to know what you dream about,
how you
    See me
If this was easy, our hearts wouldn't feel
a thing.

So bring on the fire,
I am here to stay.

Dried out heart.

Premature love grows in my garden full
of death,
The crows cry, the crows cry, *the crying*
crows.

Scarlet secrets, overflowing, swimming
in my mind.
The crows cry, the crows cry, *the crying*
crows.

Ruby scars remind me of the formless
chaos we share.
The crows cry, the crows cry, *the crying*
crows.

A child's thoughts.

I want a taste of your skin
Under the Wolf Sun.
I want the thoughts that sit
Inside your head.
I want the scent that
Illuminates from your
Broken inspiration.

My discomfort sits upon your lips.
You speak and all I hear is nonsense-
When your mouth opens you should talk
sweet love and innocence
but all you do is fill my mind with SHIT.

and

I CAN'T TAKE IT

I want out. I just need to breathe.

My lungs have turned a charcoal kind of
Green and I can hear my mother
Screaming my name from here,

"VICTORIA MARIE...."

I know I'm fucked,
I fucked up.
This is fucked up
I just can't take the pain; I can't take the
stubborn silence anymore.
You have sucked my soul dry and now it
is my time to find
The thoughts that have lived in my brain

Dreaming during the Day.

No one cares what you think when the
pavement sinks And the phone doesn't
dial.
Take my thoughts, Eat my eyes but
don't burn my Coyote Heart.
Darker than the Full Moon we married
under, Our thoughts float into oblivion.

Pocket poem 0069.

when my mother found out
I stole my cat's teeth
and
kept them in a jar,
she took
away my guitar
for years and
now she won't
let me eat snow

846 poem

days like today
i want to keep forever
hide them away in a pocket
for another day-

i want to remember what today
tastes like and how it looks
through morning eyes-

Should ~~we go~~ back?

I thought we had something
 I saw light in your eyes
And I can't even call you home
Even though I did
   I almost said accidentally
But let's be honest here
It wasn't on accident
When I see you everything
Rushes in like the sea
On a storm day, *a raw state.*
   Feelings rolling in....
Harder and harder and higher
And they are there.
No one can hide it
  We can't break the rules
But didn't we already cross the
Street together
When you started to knock?
   You knocked and I am fucked
For letting you in
For even answering the door-
Part of me hopes this is the old us
I want to be your friend
But with our powers
With our beings
   ~~- our SOULS~~
Is that possible?

But the other part of me wants
To be your life -
I want to feel us again,
I want to feel alive
And I'm sorry but you were
The only human to show me
The Moon on a rainy night.

And I crave that feeling
Every Fucking Day-

Or are we just lost lovers
On Earth walking bare footed
To find each other again (?)

Time withers

My eyelids hide the secrets we keep
from our mothers.
Peel my skin back like the orange, suck
my thoughts dry.
As mesmerizing as her pale skin may
be, always remember
The color of the midnight sky.

little

As she walks across the water, nothing
but
Pastel love sinks to the bottom,
Where the water snakes dance
And the sea turtles sleep. Water
Is no color but all the colors at once.

i will set fire to everything i see
since everything here does not
make sense to me

Bees are productive

I don't understand
Why shoes have
Laces if the human
Wearing the shoe
Is as lazy as a
Bee

lilac dreams

These feelings
...I must confess

Make me cry in the
Dead of winter

Make me shiver in the
River on a July night

Make me dance in the
Rain during a spring thunderstorm

I just want to taste the inside of
Your brain, see where you go when you
Sleep

I want to watch the love inside your
indigo
Heart grow

Beneath all things,

Deeper than

A soul can shine

I must confess...

I will love you, until the end of time.

thoughts, somewhere.

like the ocean tide
i slowly breathe in
and out
with the dawn's sun I wake before the
rest

Smaller than.

Her hair dances like the branches of my
birch tree.
Soft and delicate like winter's snow, I
hear her breathe.
To me, nothing seems more beautiful
than a smile on a woman's soul.

Take a knife to
The right eye
Chaos chases
The men
Who don't
Cry
Even when
The rain falls
In spring
Together
We can hear
Our gardens
Grow

Nothing can ever live
In this space ever again
Trashed beyond
Belief
Embarrassed to say
These are all my
Thoughts... scattered
Across the hardwood floor
Embarrassed to admit
I don't feel a goddamn thing
About this.

Lines of nonsense in America

As far as the eye can see
The light in the middle of night
Awaken, a golden hue
Before midnight only the dawn can
Taste her scent. Taken in by the beauty,
Surround the evening with
~~Mischief and coyote blood~~
for him only to lick the wounds
Never forget,
He is the one who holds your soul

shouldn't

I shouldn't have to admit
The light from the moon
Gives me a feeling of regret

great feeling of remorse
like I killed a dead horse
nothing compares to the
air on the mountaintop

peaches tumble down the
hill, where we used to kiss
where we used to dance
before the men mowed
the lawn
before I fell from the fourth
floor

before I felt death
at
my
front
door

~~cut her free~~

It can't work if we don't have time
Take my eyes,
                take my ears
I can still hear
    I can still see
I know you don't care,
                I know your
Mother wouldn't mind
Just kill me here, with the knife
That you lick at night

Inside my brain, living and hanging
Flies, withering away
Trying to make sense of this love
That you claim to give me

The sun has set
  In my beautifully broken heart
I can't help what has happened
Or what will become-
I can help myself,
  and be
            h a p p y
.....About that.

        We can dance in the sun,
Swim in the river all the way to the
Moon.
But only if you want-
Nothing but our souls on.
Organic love will then take my body-
Take control.

I have to hold on for life. I need to
breathe
Some fresh air again. I can't seem to fit
This shell that I'm in.
As the funeral begins, please hold my
Dead body up to the sky,

As the ashes need to rise and
The clouds will eat my eyes.

the 10AM BLUES

to dress my darling in the most
luscious pelt coat is an
understatement
for my feelings
towards this year.
while monkeys have been flying,
vibrating, through the placid sky,
we hear the neighbors ramble their
soothing grace while harvesting
the midnight crop.
fragments of you,
fragments of i,
elongate over
centuries of time.

Cavernous: the soul of this Child.

Drinking the high seas, with the devil
on my shoulder
I proceed to dance.
The Wolf Moon:
  our silent landscape covered in snow.
As the river freezes over, an acorn
drops.

pocket poem #421

if i told you a flower could bloom
after midnight would you believe me?

pocket poem #422

past the sea, the rivers meet.
sundrops touch my delicate skin.
to finally breathe in my own body.
again.

(TAYLOR'S HOMEWORK)

WE NEED...
Feed empathy
To the children
Who sip the river
Water to survive-
Who can't spend a dime,
Saving all just to get by.
A place
AMERICA
Can recycle her sins.
Licking bullets,
Only to let in -
The hatred
Towards men,
Towards women,
Children, animals.
Bring back the life
Of love and
Sunlight for the world
Has been in the dark
For far too long
& she can't take it
JUSTICE FOR ALL

With LOVE.

Pollinate our love,
Shower emotion over us.
Rain pours and rushes in-
The walls melt, the room
Spins & I begin to forget
My reason & the name my
Mother gave me.
Take my dreams & hold them.

....

I keep a basket near my bed at night for
all my dreams/
Good and bad/ I keep a notebook near
my heart all the time/
Black Ink, Blue Ink/ Crisp newspapers
near my soul/ Pour
The months into a cup and let them
choose/ Me or You/ You or I/

Loose Tooth.

Consider the inside of a skeleton's mind,
where glass shatters
And crows laugh. There is no such thing
as time, and the sky
Is always black. When it's mad, the
pianos catch fire and the
Crows begin to lose their feathers. Here
you are, inside the
Mind of Victoria.

Can't make sense of this river anymore.
The distant light rises above all before the storm rolls in.
The Sun will shine today after the grass grows a bit and the birds sing.
Meet us for the evening fire dance,
before the Wolf Moon,

you and I.

Lines.

Tomorrow is another day, full of
surprises and half eaten peaches.
We can't live for the future if we
can't live for today.
Take two steps back before you walk
into Winter.

North Star Love.

A twinkle in her eye.
Seashells for ears.
She loves you deeper than
The Grand Canyon and
Softer than a flower's petal.

Cursive mind.

Murder the night with your mysterious
eyes.
While dawn creeps through the
window,
The hardwood floor still smells like your
Perfume.
Our love we made is scattered on the
bedroom floor.

Skin of a kiwi.

Kiss me into the night
Arms wider than the sea
Fall into my heart
With every beat and breath
Your words I fall for
Before I hit the ground
Hold my head up
For the rough weather is
Coming

the third pocket poem

into this forest i will go

to lose my mind and
share a smile with a soul

elegance in the eye of the woman.

as I'm watching the ice melt, the ideas
sink, the minds think.
I see death in the distance, but he can't
take me yet.
There are too many flowers in my
garden that seem dead.
Roses will lay me to rest, before the sea
sweeps me away.

delicate ocean sand.

Waltzing across the ocean's surface, a Dainty Lady,
Her legs like tree limbs: strong, durable and rooted.
Around her neck hangs a Golden Heart Locket.
Rings on each finger and a soul full of truth.

Clarity

Days are for new beginnings, the start to
something different.
Different keys open my house, every day
the rain pours down.
Down where the river meets the earth,
beyond our reach.

wishes.

Drop your anchor on his ankle, nothing
feels better.
The funeral just started, and the baby
won't stop laughing.
Feel the souls comb through the room,
one by one.

Finger to the brain

Hate to the head

Fill my soul

With broken glass

Shattered

Glass slivers

Can't feel my fingers

Numb

The dried flowers cover

My heart,

Melting

Into ~~time~~

That we shared

That we once *loved*

Before a time

before the summer took you from me

I can't hold my breath much longer

For the pain in my neck

has brought tears

To my toes and my

Mother is S I C K

Of this shit I told her was *love*

She asked me to call her when it was

all said and

Done

She can't stand

to see

Her daughter eat the dirt

Too many times

Enough times to turn into

~~The EARTH~~

...

can't find the *stars on the moon*

and

that seems to be my problem

Three questions I just asked.

How do I exit a period of time
Without brushing my teeth against
The horrible things you have said?

How does one eat when their fingers
Have no feeling and their mind has
Been fried?

Where does time go when
The children are at home and the
Horses haven't been fed?

another back pocket poem

Ocean drop, sweet sun bliss. Over the
Mountains we can see this.
Everything is the way it is because of
humans. And the universe isn't equal.
Pull together the currents from your
seas, I will bring my bees.
Let's set them free, to the sunrise and
the salty breeze.

cabin in the CT woods.

Into the mountains,
Isolated.
A deep, northern numb.
An overcast sky,
    An overcast mind.
Her opaline eyes meet mine.
Slipping into a dreary
    Dream.
Where desolate
Roads warm my frigid heart.
A Bleak Connecticut Sky.

This turned awful, quick

How about the time we ate
The night, we fell asleep in your car
Only to wake up to a moose
Knocking on our door
When you fed him the news
  Only to come back and ask for more
When you give a loose tooth to
A naked whore
Only ~~God~~ can tell you
    What happens next.....

brittle bones

When your body is too weak to carry
His sins. When the love from your
Sour soul hurts to give.
Your heart weeps at the
Foot of his bed.
        A dozen dead roses
To put him to rest.

cucumbers

Eating the dirt from my shoes.
Selling my soul for used books.
When the music stops, the
            End is creeping up.
Follow your Winter Heart:
            Graceful and elegant.
Shimmer in the dark.
Acting like a child, my heart
Sings for miles.
            Nothing here to feel.

Scattered brain, scattered me.

Kiss me on the mouth,
Before the berries ripen
And the ice melts my
Cold soul. December is
A nice time of year to
Wear your thoughts.

Stolen souls.

I'd love to touch your lips in the dead
of winter.
    Pray with me:
    The wind erases my soul and gives
me
A new one. No holes, no feelings.
        BRAND   N E W.
An act of kindness? I sure don't know.

The winter stole my old soul and I ain't
complaining.

853.

Plant your seeds of love
Inside my eyes
For fall has arrived
And the grass is dead.
The sound the sun
Makes when it rains.
When there is no
Sea for us to swim in,
Take my heart and
Bury my brains-
The rest is not
Worth it.

IXI

Dry out my bones &
Hang my heart to rest/
With every sunset, my
Eyes seek forgiveness/

Throw me, bare feet and all
into an ocean of dreams.

SMALL or BIG

Nothing compares to organic love.

a hazy crescent moon.

Despite all this rain, my heart sits in my hand-
    Patiently awaiting the touch of your porcelain skin.
I will love you as my days grow older. As my mind's thoughts
    Are caught in the ocean's tide only to untangle the time
We lost dancing with angels. We will love until gold bleeds from our eyes.

slipped on a candlestick

might be sick
might be dead

can't take the lies anymore
can't take the voices
that told me so

i just want to breathe
the air again

i know that she's love

i want to feel whole

just one more time,
again.

The very middle

It makes my skin itch
And my eyes bleed

I can't stand the room
When you stand in
The very middle

My heart begins to scream
And my fingers turn green

I can't stand the room

THE UNOFFICIAL END TO THE END.

Dead bones, dry as a desert.

Skin with wrinkles, old as three
centuries.

Rugged nails, coffee stained teeth.

Eyes lay low, bloodshot.

Fire is going but I see no flame.

| BIO |

~~Victoria~~, Torrye, *Toria*, LaFlamme is a strange human who lives in the woods somewhere in Connecticut. She likes to play with earthworms, go for hikes and listen to music. When she grows u p , she wants to be an entomologist. Her first published poem, "I am a Child" was featured in *America's Emerging Poets 2018: Northeast Region*. A year later, "Centuries without Peonies" was featured in *Connecticut's Best Emerging Poets 2019: An Anthology*. And in late 2019, her first collection of nonsense was published, *I Think I've Been Here Before.*

www.ingramcontent.com/pod-product-compliance
Ingram Content Group UK Ltd.
Pitfield, Milton Keynes, MK11 3LW, UK
UKHW041955190726
13854UKWH00005B/1990